Published by Letts Educational
The Chiswick Centre
414 Chiswick High Road
London W4 5TF
020 89963333
020 87428390
mail@lettsed.co.uk
www.letts-education.com

Letts Educational is part of the Granada Learning Group.
Granada Learning is a division of Granada plc.

First published 2003

ISBN 184085 8885

All web addresses are correct at the time of going to press. The information in this book has been thoroughly researched and checked for accuracy. Safety advice is given where appropriate. Neither the authors nor the publishers can accept responsibility for any loss or damage incurred as a result of this book.

British Library Cataloguing in Publication Data
A catalogue record for this book is available from the British Library.

Acknowledgements
The publishers would like to thank the following for permission to use copyright material. Every effort has been made to trace copyright holders and to obtain their permission for the use of copyright material. The author and publishers will gladly receive information enabling them to rectify any error or omission in subsequent editions.

Commissioned by Helen Clark
Project management by Vicky Butt
Editorial by Kearsey & Finn Limited
Design and production © Gecko Limited, Bicester, Oxon
Illustrations by © Gecko Limited, Bicester, Oxon
Production by PDQ
Printed and bound by Ashford Colour Press

Introducing *Red Hot Maths Websites*

The internet is a fantastic resource for you as a Key Stage 3 maths student. Your teacher knows this – which is why you have a copy of this book.

Red Hot Maths Websites contains directions to the best sites to help you with your maths lessons. You can either use the book by yourself or ask your teacher which sites to visit and when to visit them.

How to use this book

The websites listed in this book have been divided into mathematical sections and topics. These match the topics you will be covering in school. At the start of each section, a 'What you need to know' page lists the key points and keywords you need to understand. You will need to keep checking the 'What you need to know' pages to get the most out of this book and the websites. The rest of the book gives information about individual websites.

You will see these icons on the pages:

This tells you how to get from the main index of each site to the page you really need. It tells you what to click.

Why should you go there? This section explains what's useful about the site.

Look at this section to discover our top tips and how to apply this website in your school work.

Here you will find details of any additional sites which deal with the same topic.

Don't take our word for it! This section lets you know what other Key Stage 3 students really thought of the site.

Get involved

If you want to give us your feedback on these sites, visit our website: www.letts-education.com/mathswebsites
Your comments will be updated each term so you can keep track of the best internet resources for you and your maths lessons.

Thank you

Many thanks to Mashell Bokhari for all her help with this book.

Using maths to solve problems

What you need to know

+ Diagrams
+ Tables
+ Explanation
+ Hypothesis
+ Conclusion

How to
use it

Look out
for

Hints

Other
links

Student
comments

Problem solving

www.harrypotterlessons.co.uk/general.htm

This is a direct link to an unofficial Harry Potter fan site. From this general page, look at the **Harry Potter Maths** section. There are lots of different worksheets to choose from so click on whatever takes your fancy.

A mixture of problems to try using lots of different skills including probability, proportion and ratio.

Some questions are quite basic and better for Year 7 while others are very demanding. You'll need to print off some of the worksheets, though, as they are not interactive. You'll also need to get your teacher to check your work as there aren't any answers.

school.discovery.com/brainboosters
An interesting site with a selection of different problems for you to try. They have already grouped them into different categories and there is a **Challenge of the Week**.

A bit confusing but I like the idea of Harry Potter in a maths lesson.

7

Problem solving

How to use it

Look out for

Hints

Other links

Student comments

www.ex.ac.uk/cimt/puzzles/puzzindx.htm

Here you are faced with a massive choice of puzzles and competitions, ranging from simple number problems to investigating shapes. Go on, have a try!

An excellent site if you really want to make yourself think! Begin with the **Quick Puzzles** where you will be given basic number questions and shape problems to solve. When your confidence increases, try the competitions – there are plenty to choose from.

Some of these are really tricky and will make your brain ache! If you like playing with shapes then try the **Tangram** puzzles or the **Pentominoes** ; both are excellent. Why not share the puzzles with your classmates – try to solve them together.

Great! Makes you think.

How to use it

 Look out for

 Hints

 Other links

 Student comments

www.stfx.ca/special/mathproblems/welcome.html

 How brave are you? From the **Table of Contents** pick a grade from 5 to 12.

 A site from Canada with some fun problems to really get you thinking. The questions are fairly short and straightforward in the Grade 5 section but watch out – Grade 12 is A-level standard.

 Although the problems are short, the answers are not! Start with Grade 5 and see how you get on, making use of the **Hints** to keep you going. Answers are supplied but try to resist the temptation unless you are really stuck.

 Perfect – easy to use, great layout and challenging.

Problem solving

Numbers and the number system

What you need to know

Place value and rounding

- Understand decimal notation
- Know how to multiply and divide by 10, 100, 1000
- Be able to order decimals
- Round numbers to the nearest 10, 100, 1000 using decimal places and significant figures

Integers and powers

- Working with negative and positive numbers
- Prime numbers
- Squares, cubes and index notation

Fractions

- Cancelling
- Equivalent
- Improper
- Multiply
- Divide
- Add
- Subtract
- Word problems

Decimals

- Ordering decimals
- Multiply
- Divide
- Add
- Subtract
- Word problems

Percentages

- Definition
- Converting between percentages, fractions and decimals
- Finding a percentage of a number
- Increase and decrease by a percentage

Ratio and proportion

- How to write a ratio
- Cancelling
- Divide a quantity by a ratio
- Links with proportion
- Use ratio to solve problems
- Links with enlargement and scale

How to use it

Look out for

Hints

Other links

Student comments

YEAR
7/8

www.mathsnet.net/intro.html

 Lots here to get lost in but don't panic. On the left-hand side find **Puzzles** then click on **Numeracy**.

 These activities won't take you very long, so do try them all. Start with **Place Value**, then practise your guessing skills on **Guess My Number**.

 This is a fairly basic set of activities to get you warmed up for the tricky stuff to come. You can get hooked playing **Simon Says** and the **Quiz** is great for testing your observation and memory skills.

 A great site with a memory quiz for Year 7. Perhaps too easy for Year 8?

Place value and rounding

11

How to use it

Look out for

Hints

Other links

Student comments

Place value and rounding

www.bbc.co.uk/education/mathsfile/index.shtml

After admiring the beard of Pythagoras (you'll learn about him later on) click **Games** then find **Rounding Off** on the big wheel.

One of the best sites on the net. An excellent place to play around with decimal places and significant figures. It is vital that you are confident with these, so do spend some time on this site.

There are three levels to choose from; it's probably best to begin with level 1. This site requires patience as it can take a while to load but it is great fun. I love the long arm, but why is Hypatia wearing a fake beard?

Does take a long time to load but the layout is great and I love the man who makes a rude noise!

How to use it

Look out for

Hints

Other links

Student comments

YEAR 7/8

www2.funbrain.com/cgi-bin/getskill.cgi

From this page type in 'place value' in the **Keyword** box. You now have four games to choose from. Or type in 'rounding' to get four games on rounding numbers.

Be warned that the questions can be quite tricky, so start with the first game unless you are feeling confident. Once you have enough correct answers you get a completed picture – maybe a funny little penguin.

If the questions are too easy or too hard, click on the boxes below your score to alter them to suit your ability. Do finish each game as something fun happens at the end!

www.learn.co.uk
Now you have worked through the three websites on place value and rounding, visit this site for a test.

Fantastic layout, easy to use.
Gets you thinking.

Place value and rounding

(13)

How to use it

Look out for

Hints

Other links

Student comments

Integers and powers

www.gomath.com

Find **Algebra Solutions**, then scroll down to **Algebra** and click on **Laws of Exponents**.

An American site, so the language may be unfamiliar but don't let this put you off. Try the **Submit** and **Practice** buttons if you are already confident in index notation. These buttons will actually solve problems for you.

Take a look at the **Mini-Lesson**. The examples should help you despite the technical words. All of the rules are covered here, so copy the key points for later use. Finally, try the worksheet; print it for that revision folder that you should be compiling.

To find a good test on this topic, visit the excellent BBC site. Choose **Number** then **Index Notation**.
www.bbc.co.uk/education/ks3bitesize

Very informative. I don't mind the American language.

How to use it

Look out for

Hints

Other links

Student comments

www.mathsyear2000.org/explorer/primes/index/html

The direct link takes you to a world of primes, factors and divisibility. Don't be scared!

Although the site is quite wordy, it is very informative. If you want to know about factors, primes and special numbers this is the best place to go. There are divisibility tests, prime number checks and even a special calculator to use!

It's probably best to think carefully about what you want to know, then print off the relevant information. The divisibility tests are really good as they are interactive and they are useful in lots of different areas of maths.

Integers and powers

How to use it

Look out for

Hints

Other links

Student comments

Integers and powers

funbrain.com/cgi-bin/getskill.cgi

From this page, type in the word 'negative' in the **Keyword** box. You are now provided with a long list of games to play.

A light-hearted look at negative and positive numbers. Lots of different games to try, so think about what you want to practise first. Use the **Easier** and **Harder** buttons to change the level of difficulty.

So many great games to play! Make sure you try a few of them. **Line Jumper** is good for playing with addition of negative numbers. **Guess the Number** is quite tricky.

16

How to use it

Look out for

Hints

Other links

Student comments

Fractions

www.learn.co.uk

From the home page click on **Key Stage 3 Mathematics**, then choose either **Fractions 1** (Year 7) or **Fractions 2** (Years 8–9).

Everything you will ever need to know on fractions with lots of worked examples and questions. Do try the **Speed test** and print the **Revision**, **Glossary** and **Summary** notes. These will be really useful for revision. Get organised – keep a folder of your revision notes.

This is one of the best sites around for revision and practice tests. The language is a bit technical but don't let that put you off, this is a thorough look at fractions that will really test you. If you can work through all of the sections on the left of the screen, then you need never fear fractions again!

Fantastic! Great for revision.

Fractions

How to use it • Look out for • Hints • Other links • Student comments

www.bbc.co.uk/education/ks3bitesize

From this page, select **Number** under the **Maths** heading, click **Go** and find **Fractions I** and **Fractions II**.

This is also one of the best sites to visit – excellent content and very easy to use. Work through the revision section making any notes you need, then try the test. Years 7 and 8 (Levels 4 and 5) should concentrate on **Fractions I** before moving on to **Fractions II** (Levels 5 and 6), probably in Year 9.

After you have tried the test, record your scores so that you can then check on your progress. Make a note of any help comments you are given. Why not print the page for your revision folder or copy the important parts?

It's wicked! It really helps you learn.

How to use it

Look out for

Hints

Other links

Student comments

Fractions

www2.funbrain.com/cgi-bin/getskill.cgi

From this page, type in the word 'fractions' in the **Keyword** box. You are now given a big list of games to play.

Lots of games to play, all based on fractions. **Fresh Baked Fractions** is for practising equivalent fractions while **Soccer Shootout** is for working on the four rules of fractions.

OK, so it isn't Playstation 2 but it beats doing all those worksheets, and think of poor little Jackson the dog, he must be starving! Remember you can change the difficulty by clicking on **Start Over** at the bottom of the screen.

Great fun. Jackson is quite cute too!

How to use it   Look out for   Hints   Other links   Student comments

ricksmath.com

 Look at the top of this home page – the choice is massive. Find the word **Decimals** and click. This is good for Years 7 and 8 as an introduction and as revision for Year 9.

 I don't know who Rick is but he is doing a great job! There are literally hundreds of worksheets for you to work through. Lots of reading first (yes, do read it!) then some good examples with clear explanations and diagrams

 It is important that you work through all of the pages so that you meet every type of decimal. There are over four pages of explanation so print them off to make it easier to read. You can then fill in the answers to the problems that Rick poses. Unfortunately no answers are supplied.

 ferl.becta.org.uk/display.cfm?catid=36&page=25&resid=2399

Choose from the menu on the left-hand side of the screen to access some Powerpoint presentations on decimals and fractions.

 Needs more colour and answers. Challenging though.

How to use it

Look out for

Hints

Other links

Student comments

YEAR
All

Decimals

www.aplusmath.com/Worksheets/index.html

 This link takes you directly to a selection of worksheets on decimals.

 Not the most exciting site in the world but if you just want to practise the four rules of decimals then this is where you need to be. The worksheets allow you to decide how easy or hard you want them to be.

 Either print the worksheets off or better still try the online exercises. These are slightly more interactive and you can have your work marked online. You will receive a mark out of 100 – a percentage score – and, more importantly, the correct answers.

 Very informative, easy to use and with a great layout. Covers everything you need for decimals.

How to use it

 Look out for

 Hints

 Other links

 Student comments

www.mathslessons.co.uk

 To find the decimal section put your mouse over the **Number** part of the menu – there's no need to click. The different topics are all displayed – click **Decimal**.

 Can this site really be free? One of the best sites around and completely interactive and colourful. Best to work your way through the pages, but if you are feeling confident, just select what you want from **Order**, **Adding**, **Multiply** and **Test**.

 All of the lessons are timed so you know you won't be there for ever. Make sure you try the test, which takes about 15 minutes to complete, recording your scores for future use. Don't forget to **Beat the Clock**, a two-minute test where you answer as many questions as possible!

 Nice layout, clear instructions, good for revision

How to use it

 Look out for

 Hints

 Other links

 Student comments

Percentages

www.aaamath.com

 This is another American site. From this page choose **Percent** from the list of maths topics.

 Plenty of quick-fire questions to sharpen your skills. This site has hundreds of pages of basic maths skills, interactive practice, an explanation of each maths topic and several challenge games on every page. **Learn** and **Practice** are still the most useful sections to use.

 The Learn section gives brief explanations of the main points you need to know. Copy these into your revision folder to refer to later. There are lots of other good things on this site, for example the **Cool!!!** section in **Explore** has some excellent links to other interesting sites.

 www.mathslessons.co.uk/lessonplans/ percentages/index.htm
Excellent explanation on a very important topic – interactive too.

 Great but where are the pictures? It looks boring but it has lots of useful information.

23

How to use it

 Look out for

 Hints

 Other links

 Student comments

www.learn.co.uk

 From the home page click on
Key Stage 3 Mathematics, then choose
Percentages.

 Probably the best site for dealing with
percentages. Everything you need is here,
whatever level you are at. The explanation is
clear and the presentation makes it easy to
read. Pick one section at a time, then try the
Exercises and the **Speed Tests**. There is also
a **Test All Levels** to try once you are confident.

 As there is so much in this site, be careful not
to try to do it all at once. Decide on what you
need first – this will depend on what year you
are in – study it, then make notes of what you
have learnt. Ask your teacher for guidance on
which sections you need.

 I love the speed tests!

How to use it

 Look out for

 Hints

 Other links

 Student comments

Percentages

www.mathgoodies.com/lessons

 Look at the **Table of Contents**, find **Understanding Percent** and click the **Shortcut**.

 Stacks of pages with lots of questions and clear explanations; certainly worth a look. Try the different sections at the bottom of each page – there are ten to look at.

 The ratio connection is worth remembering. Copy out the table to help. Do try the puzzles and exercises connected to percentages; they are all interactive giving you immediate feedback.

Ratio and proportion

 How to use it

 Look out for

 Hints

 Other links

 Student comments

www.mathslessons.co.uk

 This is a useful site for Levels 5 and 6. Put your mouse over the **Number** part of the menu – no need to click. The different topics are all displayed – click **Ratio** then **Tutorial** to get started.

 An excellent site with lots of clear explanations. There are three sections to choose from, so do them in order starting with **Sharing**. Work your way through the pages (the easiest way is to use the arrows on the bottom left-hand side) then try to **Beat the Clock** for a two-minute test (click on the clock on the left to activate it).

 Each of the three pages has its own questions. Click on **Next** to see them. Do at least five on each page plus the two-minute end-of-topic test. There are also three worksheets for you to download and print off – they're not interactive but still worth having.

 www.bized.ac.uk/virtual/economy/policy/outcomes/debt
A real-life activity on debt ratio and the economy.

 Easy to understand and to find your way around.

26

How to use it

Look out for

Hints

Other links

Student comments

www.mathsisfun.com

On the left-hand side of the home page, choose **Number & Algebra** then click **Ratio**. This activity is good for Levels 5–6.

Chocolate crispies! This is a bit of fun but first use your ratio skills to work out the ingredients. Maths and food, surely a winning combination.

A 'real-life' activity to make use of your maths. Follow the links to actually make the chocolate crispies – then share them with friends.

Helps you understand ratio.

Ratio and proportion

How to use it

 Look out for

 Hints

 Other links

 Student comments

Ratio and proportion

www.bbc.co.uk/education/ks3bitesize

 From this page you select **Number**, click **Go** and find **Ratio and unitary method**. Again, this is a good page for Levels 5–6.

 As always, the content is great. Plenty of good, clear explanation on the different sorts of ratio questions you could be asked. No wonder it is one of the most visited maths sites on the net. Go through the revision section first – there are five sections to work through – then try a test.

 Take note of the **Wise Up** and **Remember** comments; there's always good advice here. Record your test score so you can go back at a later date, do the test again and monitor your progress. You could also print a copy of the test for later exam revision.

 Wicked site! Helps revision and tests your brain. Fantastic layout.

Algebra

What you need to know

Equations
- Use letters to represent unknown numbers
- Construct and solve equations
- Substitution
- Simplifying
- Trial and improvement

Formulae
- Substitution
- Expression
- Variable
- Derive a formula
- Change the subject

Sequences
- Patterns
- Term
- n^{th} term
- Special sequences (square, triangular, Fibonacci)

Graphs
- Co-ordinates
- Quadrants
- Axes
- Straight-line graphs
- Gradient
- Intercept
- Real-life graphs

How to use it

Look out for

Hints

Other links

Student comments

www.algebrahelp.com

The world of algebra at your fingertips! Look at 'What you need to know' on page 29 and chec for those topics on the site. You may need to scroll down to **Lessons**.

Very wordy, but the **Worksheets** section is good f practice and definitely worth a look. Go to **Lesson** and begin with **Equation Basics**, then click on **Worksheets** to practise on some questions.

The lessons section might be worth printing off, otherwise make use of the worksheets and definitely check out the **Equation Calculator** – what a great idea! The **Resources** section also has some interesting aspects which are worth a look. Do you want to know all the primes from 1 to 100?

www.learn.co.uk/default.asp?WCI=Topic&WCU=3961

Two tests for you to try after you have worked through these three equations websites.

Not very attractive but has some great information. I like the Equation Calculator.

How to use it

 Look out for

 Hints

 Other links

 Student comments

Equations

www.gomath.com

 Click **Algebra Solutions**, scroll down to **Algebra**, then find **Solving Equations With One Variable**.

 Some good explanations here with lots of opportunities to perfect your skills. You have to be confident working with equations, so it is worth spending time in this site. Click **Practice** to try some examples or enter your own equation and click **Submit** to see it solved – handy for checking your equation homework!

 Once you have had a little practice, try a **Mini-Lesson** or a **Worksheet**. Best to print the worksheet, solve the equations then click the answer button to check your answers. If you are stuck, go back and make use of the Submit button.

 Good explanations. The worksheets are useful too.

How to use it | Look out for | Hints | Other links | Student comments

www.mathslessons.co.uk

 Put your mouse over the **Algebra** section then click **Solving Equations**.

 This site never fails to produce the goods – colourful, interactive and, best of all, easy to understand. Click **Tutorial** to get started. Work your way through the **Equations Lessons** (it takes about 20–30 minutes if you do it properly) copying the useful bits as you go. There are ten pages plus a test and each page gives you questions to solve.

 You must visit this site! It will help you, especially with revision. After you have worked through the ten pages and the test, remember to click the clock on the left to try the two-minute timed test. By then you will be an expert at solving equations.

 I really love this site. Lessons are cool and I am going to use this site for my own revision.

How to use it

Look out for

Hints

Other links

Student comments

Formulae

www.easymaths.com/algebra_main.htm

Visit this page and enter the world of algebra. Best to start at the top and work your way down.

An excellent site with friendly language to explain what is going on in probably the hardest part of your maths. The topics covered here go all the way to Year 11 so don't panic, you can ignore the really hard stuff for now.

Although this is an excellent site, it is very wordy, so don't try to read it all at once. It also lacks questions for you to try, so once you have worked through the explanations and examples, visit the sites on the next two pages of this book to practise what you have learnt.

www.adamzone.co.uk/formulae.htm
Some good explanation on how to
Change the Subject of a Formula.

Hallelujah! I actually understand what it's trying to say. Cool site, loads of information.

How to use it

Look out for

Hints

Other links

Student comments

aaamath.com/equ.html

The title **About Equations** does look a little scary! Just choose
Evaluating Expressions with One Variable.

A colourful site with lots of good features, although more pictures would help. Look at the top of the screen and choose **Practice** for questions on substitution problems.

The questions are a little repetitive but they are fine for practising substitution. Do try the
Evaluating Expressions with Two Variables as well.

How to use it

Look out for

Hints

Other links

Student comments

www.mathgoodies.com/lessons

The link takes you to a Table of Contents listing lessons for you to try. Choose **Topics in Pre-Algebra** and click under **Description**. Now click **Writing Algebraic Expressions**.

A fairly straightforward site with language that is easy to understand. The examples of algebraic expressions are especially helpful. By clicking on key words you get pop-up boxes which give you definitions – copy these for later use.

Read through the explanation and examples then try the **Exercises**. You get immediate feedback to help correct any mistakes. Other sections are offered at the end of the test – try the **Pre-Algebra Puzzles** for a bit of fun.

Easy to understand with great definitions.

How to use it

Look out for

Hints

Other links

Student comments

Sequences

www.bbc.co.uk/education/ks3bitesize

This is good for Levels 4–6. Make sure **Algebra** is in the maths subject box, then click **Go**.

Look at **Number Patterns I** and **Number Patterns II** for a good introduction to the special sequences that you need to know. It also covers the tricky n^{th} term. Use the revision section first, where you will meet square, cube and triangular numbers. You can probably ignore the even and odd number sequences.

Make notes as you work through the revision pages, or print them off, then tackle the tests. The nth term is very important and Year 9 pupils will face it in their SATs. Look at the other topics here in the algebra section – they are also excellent.

www.cut-the-knot.com/Curriculum/index.shtml
A site full of activities that really make you think. Scroll down to see the full list.

Cool site. I love the revision pages. Wicked layout.

How to use it

Look out for

Hints

Other links

Student comments

www.learn.co.uk

 Useful for Levels 3–6 (Years 7 and 8) and Levels 5–8 (Years 8 and 9). From the home page click on **Key Stage 3 Mathematics**, then choose **Sequences and Patterns** in the **Algebra** section.

 One of the most popular sites as it always gives clear explanations with added interactive features. Work through the first four sub-topics on the left-hand side of your screen, trying the questions as you go. Ignore the quadratic function section for now.

 Everything you need on sequences is here, plus stuff you don't need – the quadratic part! Remember to do the **Tests** too as this is the best way to check your understanding. There are lots of different sequences, so remember to copy out the definitions the site gives you.

 Nice layout, clear instructions. Very useful tests. Too much info – my brain is hurting!

Sequences

How to use it Look out for Hints Other links Student comments

www.eastmaths.com/how_to_
succeed_with_maths.htm

This direct link takes you to a page all about sequences.

Just some information to work through here but it gives some helpful guidance on the nth term.

Make notes or print the page. There's also lots of advice in other parts of the site.

A little boring but has some useful information.

How to use it

 Look out for

 Hints

 Other links

 Student comments

www.mathslessons.co.uk

 Go to **Algebra** then click on **Co-ordinates**. You now have two options – take the **Lesson** or play the game **Connect 4**.

 Connect 4 is great fun but you need a partner to play against. You get to practise logical thinking and your co-ordinate skills – and of course have a little fun at the same time.

 Now you are an expert at Connect 4, why not try **Connect 5**? This is much harder as you are now using all four quadrants, which will also help you when dealing with negative numbers.

 exploremath.com
Graphically, this is one of the best sites around. Click on one of five little graphs to get started.

How to use it   Look out for   Hints   Other links   Student comments

www.mathsonline.co.uk

 Unfortunately, you have to pay for this site to get full access but the free stuff is superb. Click on the picture of the old man in the bath, which should be on the left-hand side of your screen.

 This activity is great fun. Once it is loaded you have control of the taps, the plug and even the old man – Archimedes! This activity gives you a look at a real-life situation: the graph shows how a bath fills with water.

 Watch the graph carefully as you put the plug in and turn the taps on and off. Can you predict what will happen to the graph? What happens if you run the bath without the plug in? Play around and give old Archimedes a bath.

 Really funny to see the hairy old man in the bath! I like the animation too.

How to use it
 Look out for
 Hints
 Other links
 Student comments

Graphs

mathforum.org/cgraph/cslope/intro.html

 This links directly to the page you need from the Math Forum site.

 A funny way of looking at lines. There are lots of pages to follow with some good advice on how to plot lines. There is a lot to work through but you can always skip pages by using the links on the left-hand side of the screen. Only the basics are needed for Years 7 and 8 but if you are in Year 9 then you need to know all about the intercept and gradient.

 There is so much here that it might be better to just look at a few pages at a time. It can also be a little complicated – note the way it finds the gradient.

 There are other ways to find the gradient – have a look at www.learn.co.uk/Algebra/Graphs where you can also try the **Test**.

Shape, space and measures

What you need to know

Angles
- Acute
- Obtuse
- Right angle
- Parallel
- Reflex
- Perpendicular
- Vertically opposite
- Alternate
- Corresponding
- Interior

Shapes
- Vertex
- Face
- Edge
- Polygon
- Interior and sum of interior angles
- Regular
- Exterior angles

Transformations
- Symmetry
- Reflect
- Rotate
- Translate

- Scale factor
- Centre of enlargement
- Scale drawings

Constructions and loc
- Protractor
- Compass
- Nets
- Mid-point
- Bisector
- Perpendicular
- Parallel

Measures
- Kilograms
- Litres
- Metres
- Temperature
- Perimeter
- Area
- Volume

Pythagoras
- Right-angled triangles
- Squaring numbers
- Hypotenuse
- Pythagorean triples

How to use it

 Look out for

 Hints

 Other links

 Student comments

www.ambleside.schoolzone.co.uk/
ambleweb/numeracy.htm

 This link leads you to a list of everything on the Ambleside site. Just scroll down to **Shape, Space and Angles** under **Tools for Teaching**. Choose from **What's My Angle?** and **Angle Activities** – both are excellent.

 This is a superb site for exploring protractors and basic angles. Although it is aimed at primary schools, this site is too good to ignore. Enjoy playing with the interactive protractor but remember we are here to learn!

 Play What's My Angle? to get a feel for size and how to use a protractor. You must practise, though, with a real protractor. Then you can try the Angle Activities. Look at angles in triangles, opposite angles and the other angles keywords listed on page 42. Make notes on your findings – lots of special angles for you to learn.

 plus.maths.org/issue7/xfile/index.html
A site which shows you how to perform constructions with angles. There's also a good link to loci. How do you trisect an angle?

How to
use it

Look out
for

Hints

Other
links

Student
comments

www.mathsisfun.com

Scroll down the homepage and click on
Shape, Space and Measures on the left-hand
side. Begin at the top and get clicking!

You are given lots of basic definitions and
simple diagrams, though they are not interactive.
Spend time working through them – use the
topics listed in 'What you need to know' on
page 42 to guide you.

You could print the pages but you are more
likely to remember the maths if you make your
own notes. Pay particular attention to the
diagrams – they are often easier to remember
than the words.

How to use it

Look out for

Hints

Other links

Student comments

www.bbc.co.uk/education/ks3bitesize

From this page, select **Shape and Space**, click **Go** and find **Angles, Parallels and Polygons**. These activities are excellent for Level 6.

As usual, the Bitesize site handles this topic very well. Work through the revision section, noting the diagrams. They are all very similar and students often get confused between corresponding, alternate and interior angles. When you have worked through them, don't forget to take the test.

Be sure to copy all important diagrams and facts – you will need them all the way through to Year 11. Print a copy of the test for your revision folder; then you can take it again as your exams approach.

I liked it. Good layout, easy to understand and the diagrams are great!

Shapes

How to use it

Look out for

Hints

Other links

Student comments

www.coolmath.com/home.htm

You need to find **Interior Angles of Regular Polygons** – it should be on the right-hand side of this page.

A very colourful site with brief, to-the-point explanations – just what we like! Although you have to pay for much of the material, the free stuff is still very good. This page has the essential facts and methods for finding the interior angles of shapes. The method of splitting shapes into triangles is really important, so remember it!

The examples take you through from polygons to hexagons. Now you should work on heptagons, octagons, nonagons and decagons. A table of your results will be very useful. Note the formula and have a go at working it out for yourself from scratch – quite a tricky task.

www.lessonplanspage.com /MathArt2D3D ShapesFromToothpicksChick-Peas48.htm
This site shows you how to explore and create 2D and 3D shapes using toothpicks and chickpeas!

A good site. I liked the explanation but the method's a bit fiddly.

How to use it

 Look out for

 Hints

 Other links

 Student comments

Shapes

www.adamzone.co.uk

 From this very personal homepage click on **The Triangle** on the left of the screen.

 Can you believe this site is written by 11-year-old Adam Spencer? Very impressive! Adam gives you 'everything you need to know about triangles'. Copy the six diagrams and their notes at the beginning of the page, then read through Adam's **Things to Remember**.

 The language used is quite simple and readable – a useful site for getting the facts. Adam does move on to Pythagoras but this is only needed for Year 9, Level 7. However, there's no harm in having a look!

How to use it

 Look out for

 Hints

 Other links

 Student comments

Shapes

www.learn.co.uk

 You probably know the route by now – **Key stage 3 Mathematics**, then click **Polygons** under the **Shape, Space and Measurement** heading.

 One of my favourite sites, as you have probably guessed by now! Work through the pages using the links given on the left-hand side of the page. The most important link is **Angles in a polygon**.

 Everything here is worth looking at. Make notes, print the pages – you need it all. Once you have worked through the main objectives, remember to do the tests. That's the best way to check your understanding.

How to use it

Look out for

Hints

Other links

Student comments

www.mathsnet.net/transform/index.html

This takes you directly to the section on Transformations. Choose from the links provided on the right-hand side of the page.

Quite an impressive site, and extremely interactive. It's probably best to work through the links in order and investigate each section. You could spend hours playing so you will need to be imaginative to get the most from your visit.

You can have great fun here but the site doesn't really explain what is going on so you'll also have to think! Go through the four stages it offers slowly; depending on where you click you get a different lesson.

www.bbc.co.uk/education/ks3bitesize/maths/home_menus/menu_shape_space.shtml
Lots of really useful material here on transformations with superb interactive diagrams.

How to use it

Look out for

Hints

Other links

Student comments

www.easymaths.com/shape_main.htm

This whole section is on shapes. You need to look at **Transform Your Abilities**.

Brief but to the point! The site gives the main details needed but not much else.

This is useful as a reminder of the key topics. Make notes on the information you are given – diagrams are essential!

www.mathsnet.net/transformations/index.html
Use the site above together with
www.easymaths.com to make it more useful.

Transformations

How to use it   Look out for   Hints   Other links   Student comments

nrich.maths.org/prime/index.htm

This site is designed for younger pupils who like to solve problems. (Years 8 and 9 should find the harder puzzles on Nrich Club.) Find **Library** on the lighthouse and click. Now choose the **Shape and Space** folder and pick some of the puzzles.

An interesting site to put your knowledge to the test. Be warned, some of the problems are very tough, even for older students! **Symmetry Grid** is a nice puzzle to get you mentally warmed up and the **Tangram** puzzles look simple but they're not!

A lovely site to play around with and it's packed with problems to solve. Don't panic, answers are always supplied. You will need to click on the different folders to find all the available puzzles.

I found the questions on this site really hard. Really made my brain work!

Transformations

51

How to use it

Look out for

Hints

Other links

Student comments

Constructions and loci

www.easymaths.com/shape_main.htm

From here find **Come On, Do the Loci-motion**.
(Are you laughing already?)

This page just offers explanations and a couple of useful diagrams, but it is very clear. Loci is a tricky topic to learn from a website – have a go

A question on Loci often comes up on SATs papers, so you need to be aware of it. Print the page but you also need to learn about constructions – see www.learn.co.uk on the next page.

www.4learning.co.uk/homework/hot_topics/hot_topics_maths.html
This is Channel 4's site and is worth a look. It features some good material on basic loci.

How to use it

 Look out for

 Hints

 Other links

 Student comments

www.learn.co.uk

 You probably know where to go by now! Just in case: **Key Stage 3 Mathematics** then **Loci** under **Shape, Space and Measurement**.

 No apologies for using this site yet again – the material here does loci so well we have to use it! As this is a tricky topic, make sure you go through each key part on the left-hand side of the screen. The goat animation in **Locus as a Path** and **Locus as a Region** works well.

 The animations are the best way to think about loci but remember that you will have to construct these diagrams using a ruler and a compass, so *practise* – it is not good enough just to see it done on the screen. What better way to check on your skills than to try the Level 5–8 test?

Constructions and loci

How to use it | Look out for | Hints | Other links | Student comments

www.adamzone.co.uk/loci.htm

This link takes you straight to where you need to be.

A clear, well-presented site with good diagrams but no animations (see the previous site for these). Use it as a reinforcement of the main points you need to know.

If you worked through the previous site, then you should just try the questions at the end of this site. If you need more explanation, then read through the information and check out the diagrams for help. Print the diagrams for your revision folder.

The diagrams are good. Maybe the layout and explanation could be improved, but then Adam is only 11. Amazing!

How to use it

Look out for

Hints

Other links

Student comments

Measures

www.bbc.co.uk/education/mathsfile/index.shtml

This site is intended for younger pupils but most people will find it fun! Choose **Games** (patience may be needed while it loads) click **Animal Weigh-in**, then choose a level.

This site is worth the wait as you get to practise metric and imperial measures in a fun way. Level 1 is straightforward but, be warned, Level 3 is very tricky. Have the sound on if possible!

This is great fun and you learn at the same time – what more could you ask for? All levels test a mixture of different units both metric and imperial – you need to know both. Enjoy it and make a few notes at the same time.

www.learn.co.uk/preparation/maths/ks2_weight/default.htm

This link actually takes you to a page which lists six of the best sites around on this topic.

How to use it   Look out for   Hints   Other links   Student comments

www.mathslessons.co.uk

Straight into **Shape** then click either **Area of Shapes** and then **Circles** (for Years 8 and 9) or **Volume of Prisms** (volume is actually easier to start with).

This site is constantly being updated and improved. It features lots of clear explanation, good diagrams, and pictures that move! The main shapes are covered and circles are dealt with extremely well, with three tests to challenge you.

Although it explains area and volume superbly, there aren't any volume questions.

For volume go to www.learn.co.uk to try some practice questions and take a test.

I really like this site. Good for making notes for revision.

How to use it

Look out for

Hints

Other links

Student comments

Measures

tqjunior.thinkquest.org/3804

From this page you are faced with five main headings: **Length**, **Volume**, **Mass**, **Temperature** and **Time**. Take a look at each of them.

This is really a reference site. If you are looking for basic facts with some history then this is a good place to visit. It supplies good converters so you can change between different units as well as providing useful background information.

To get the best from this site, ask yourself a question, then use the converter to check your answer. For example, what is 45 °F in Celsius? Copy the main conversions as they are essential. The Time section is the best of the lot.

How to use it

Look out for

Hints

Other links

Student comments

www.mathslessons.co.uk

Put the mouse over **Shape**, find **Pythagoras** and click.

You are given a choice of a **Tutorial** or a **Game**. Take the tutorial first, we'll play the game later! It's no surprise that this site teaches the topic so well. Just follow the instructions carefully and think about the questions they ask you. The tutorial will take about 20 minutes to work through.

These pages explain why Pythagoras is so important to mathematicians. It's a good idea to copy the **Summary** on page 8 then do the two tests supplied. Finally, as a reward for your hard work, you get to play the **Pythagoras Millionaire** game – enjoy it!

How to use it

 Look out for

 Hints

 Other links

 Student comments

www.bbc.co.uk/schools/gcsebitesize/
maths/shapeih/index.shtml

 Click **Revise** next to **Pythagoras' Theorum**.

 As this is for Years 10 and 11, there are more words and less pictures! But the explanation is quite clear and easy to follow with examples to help your understanding. There are only two pages to work through followed by a test to check that you have really learnt it.

 As there is rather a lot of explanation you should print off the pages to keep for revision. The **Test Bite** test is interactive so you can check your answers straight away and try again if you make mistakes. You should now be an expert on Pythagoras. Just to be sure, on the next site there are some real exam questions for you to try.

How to use it

Look out for

Hints

Other links

Student comments

www.4learning.co.uk/netnotes/dsp_
series.cfm?programid+1516

This is the learning website from Channel 4.
Use the menu on the left to navigate the
Pythagoras pages.

This site is designed to be used alongside a
television programme on Pythagoras but you
can still use it without the programme. Go to
Key Facts and Exam Tips first as this tells about
the theorem, then look at the **Worksheets** for
some practice.

Although this site isn't interactive, as a resource
for questions it is excellent, so do print the
worksheets off. Note the exam questions it gives;
these are actual GCSE questions for Year 11 so if
you can do these you are doing very well!

For more information on this great man take a
look at this site.
www-history.mcs.st-and.ac.uk/Mathematicians/
Pythagoras.html
You can also look at page 76 of this book.

Handling data

What you need to know

Averages
+ Data
+ Mean
+ Mode
+ Median
+ Range
+ Discrete
+ Continuous

Graphs and charts
+ Tally
+ Frequency table
+ Bar chart
+ Pie chart
+ Pictogram

+ Histogram
+ Frequency polygon
+ Scatter graph

Probability
+ Chance
+ Impossible
+ Certainty
+ Random
+ Possible outcomes
+ Independent
+ Mutually exclusive
+ Relative frequency

Averages

How to use it

Look out for

Hints

Other links

Student comments

www.mathsisfun.com

Click **Handling Data** on the left-hand side. You then have the top three sections to choose from – take your pick from **Mean**, **Median** or **Mode** – it doesn't matter which average you do first.

A great site to remind yourself which average is which. Read through the three sections to jog your memory. You have to be confident about how to work out the mean, mode and median and about which average to use in certain conditions.

When you have read through the mean, median and mode, make brief notes from the site for future use. It is very easy to get the three averages confused.

www.censusatschool.ntu.ac.uk/default.asp
This site provides lots of real-life data and an online census for you to take part in.

I found the site a little confusing but the notes are helpful.

How to use it

Look out for

Hints

Other links

Student comments

www.bbc.co.uk/education/ks3bitesize

From this page you select **Handling Data**, click **Go** and find **Comparing Distributions/Measures of Average**.

You should be familiar with this site by now – it is always worth checking out, whatever the topic. Go through the revision section first to make sure you know your averages then try the test. Pay attention to the **Wise Up** section.

The five sections here should clear up any problems you may have. Note that the range is not an average. It measures the spread of your data. The test only covers Levels 4–5.

To tackle the higher levels, try www.learn.co.uk for some harder questions.

How to use it

Look out for

Hints

Other links

Student comments

www.mathgoodies.com/lessons/vol8/range.html

This link takes you to the first of several lessons on range.

The site gives you basic definitions with a few examples followed by a short interactive test. The feedback is immediate, so use this to sort out any problems you might be having. At the end of this page you get nine options to choose from – make sure you visit the three on averages.

The explanations are good – print them off for your revision folder. Note that there is a worksheet section. You have to print these as they are not interactive, but answers are supplied. If you are in Year 9 you also need to visit the section on **Advanced Mean**.

How to use it

 Look out for

 Hints

 Other links

 Student comments

Graphs and charts

> www.mathleague.com/help/data/data.htm

 You should see a list of different types of chart under the heading **Using Data and Statistics**. Click on your choice or just scroll down.

 Perhaps not the most exciting site to look at but it gives examples of each type of chart that you need to understand together with some explanation.

 It is a good idea to print off the three charts: **Line Graphs** , **Pie Charts** and **Bar Graphs** for your revision folder. Take note: you also need to put angles on pie charts.

 Stuck with this or any other topic? Then visit this link where you can get your questions answered:
www.4learning.co.uk/apps/homework/maths/index.jsp

How to use it

Look out for

Hints

Other links

Student comments

Graphs and charts

www.learn.co.uk

As usual: Key Stage 3 Mathematics then choose Handling Data and click Presenting Data.

More superb material to actively work through – the best way to learn. Use the links on the left-hand side of the screen to decide what you need to focus on. The topics here will last you almost to Year 11, so take your time, you don't have to know it all now.

There's so much excellent material here that you might almost say there is too much! You don't need all the charts, so just check each topic as you cover it at school. For your SATs, concentrate on the 'What you need to know' points listed on page 61 of this book. The test provided cover Levels 3–8 so there is something for everyone.

How to use it

 Look out for

 Hints

 Other links

 Student comments

www.bbc.co.uk/education/mathsfile/index.shtml

 Select **Games** then find **Data Picking** on the big wheel – remember to be patient.

 This is such a funny site that we have to use it again if only for the sound effects! Choose your level – Level 1 for Year 7 and so on. Level 1 uses pie charts, Level 2, grouping data and Level 3, scatter graphs.

 Amusing, interactive and educational. Note the **Key Ideas** and **Tips**. The Key Ideas are really good as they give the main points you need to know. Print them for your revision folder.

 This is the site with the funny noises! I really liked this one.

Probability

 How to use it

 Look out for

 Hints

 Other links

 Student comments

www.mathslessons.co.uk

 Under **Data**, find **Probability**.

 An excellent introduction to probability. Even if you know a little about probability you should still look at the material here. It's colourful, interactive and there aren't too many words.

 Work your way through the pages on **Simple Probability**, trying all of the questions. The section on simple probability is for everyone but if you want to push yourself further (Year 9) take a look at the next section and **Rule**. This is much harder and is for those aiming for Level 7 in their SATs.

 This page offers links to six of the best sites around on data handling.
www.learn.co.uk/preparation/maths/datahandling/default.htm

 I love this site.
A fun and easy way of learning.

www.adamzone.co.uk/probability.htm

 This link takes you straight to where you need to be.

 This is actually a GCSE site but still it's useful for Key Stage 3. Read through and make notes from all the useful explanations. The key points you need are in the first few sections; for now you can ignore the last part on dependent events.

 The site isn't very interactive but the explanation is clear and the examples are good. Make sure you do the questions right at the end of the site.

How to
use it

Look out
for

Hints

Other
links

Student
comments

www.mathgoodies.com/lessons

From this homepage you should see a
Table of Contents. Click the **Probability**
shortcut.

The site begins with a gentle introduction to
simple probability. Do look at the experiments
and especially note the language. There are
questions for you to answer at the end and
they are marked immediately, so you can
check on your understanding.

If you don't need the explanations that are
offered, go straight to the questions at the
bottom of the page. Now notice all the other
sections they give you, for example
Sample Spaces, which sounds tricky but is
very well explained. There are also worksheets
to print for your revision folder.

How to use it

Look out for

Hints

Other links

Student comments

Puzzles

---

www1.tpgi.com.au/users/puzzles

 Click on the big arrow labelled **Quick Index**. You will be offered a huge range of puzzles to choose from.

 An excellent site if puzzles are your thing. You will need to spend some time exploring the puzzles and thinking about what you want to practise. **Minimentals** will help with mental addition and subtraction whereas **Harder** will test multiplication and division. They are all really good, and perfect for sharpening your mental and logic skills.

 Although it is a good idea to print the puzzles off so that you can complete them at your leisure, the interactive puzzles can be completed online. You can time yourself or challenge a friend to complete the puzzle in the fastest time. All answers are included and the interactive puzzles will also give you hints.

 puzzlemaker.school.discovery.com
Here you can create your own puzzles, from crosswords to word searches. You need never be bored again!

Puzzles

How to
use it

Look out
for

Hints

Other
links

Student
comments

www.nrich.maths.org.uk

Look to the left-hand side of your screen then click on **Problems**.

The aim of this site is to make you think. You don't have to be brilliant at maths to tackle the problems but be prepared to spend plenty of time thinking about each of them. They get harder as you work down the list.

Start by choosing problems at the beginning of the list – **Penta Problems** is good to get you going. Clues are supplied if you get stuck, so use these before giving in and looking at the answers! It is better to do just a few problems thoroughly rather than half finish lots of them.

How to use it
 Look out for
 Hints
 Other links
 Student comments

Puzzles

homepage.powerup.com.au/~rdale/maths.htm

 This link takes you straight to the index page. The index is grouped by school year and links you to lots of other pages.

 This is an excellent site as it gives you links to a variety of puzzles and problems, which are mostly colourful, fun and interactive. Don't worry about the year groups listed – this is just a general guide to how difficult the problems are.

 As with previous puzzle sites, try the problems from the sections at the beginning first. A+ Maths is very good for number work, Tangrams is excellent for shape work. Perimeter to the Max is enjoyable and you get some free software to download too.

Puzzles

www.censusatschool.ntu.ac.uk/quizpuzzle.asp

 Look to the left side of your screen to find six choices. The last three are the puzzles.

 This puzzle page is from the Census at School website, which is excellent, so do explore the site as well as playing with these puzzles. The **Memory Puzzle** obviously tests your memory! The **Slide Puzzle** is a classic puzzle based on logic and strategy and the **Word Search** is based on the handling data keywords.

 The Slide Puzzle, despite being a really old puzzle, is excellent. To really get to grips with the handling data keywords, print the word search then complete it. How many of the keywords can you explain? Go and research the ones you can't explain!

How to use it

Look out for

Hints

Other links

Student comments

Puzzles

www.schoolzone.co.uk/students/
learninggame/learninggameindex.htm

You can see the index of all the games, so click (Maths) for now; you can try the other subjects later.

This is a newly re-launched site packed with useful information on all your subjects. It will link you to other recommended sites where you can choose from all the best online games; some you will have met already, others will be new to you.

With so many games to play, you could be here a while! The (Baseball) game is great for practising your tables. The (BBC Online) games are always good; (Bargains Galore) is great fun if you are in Year 7.

Famous mathematicians: Pythagoras

How to use it · Look out for · Hints · Other links · Student comments

www.mathsyear2000.org/explorer/
mathematicians/pythagoras.shtml

This link takes you straight to the Pythagoras page.

Here you will find general information about who Pythagoras was and why he is famous. There are links at the bottom of the page that will take you to other more mathematical sites about Pythagoras, which are good for revision purposes.

It might be interesting to build up a folder on the great mathematicians, so print this page off. Visit www-groups.dcs.st-and.ac.uk/~ history/Posters2/Pythagoras.html for a picture of Pythagoras.

Visit the site below to enter the
Hall of Great Mathematicians.
www.siue.edu/~dcollin/mathfame.html

How to use it

 Look out for

 Hints

 Other links

 Student comments

www-groups.dcs.st-and.ac.uk/~history/Mathematicians/Einstein.html

 This link takes you straight to the Einstein page.

 A very detailed site about one of the cleverest men there has ever been. Even though it is rather wordy, stick with it as Einstein was a fascinating man. He wasn't a great pupil, though, and even failed some of his exams! There are lots of pictures to look at as well.

 There's too much here to print for your folder on great mathematicians so make your own notes then print a few of the photos. Be sure to get some of his quotes too, such as, 'Do not worry about your difficulties in mathematics, I assure you that mine are greater.' It's encouraging to know that even great minds struggle with maths!

Famous mathematicians: Einstein

77

How to use it

 Look out for

 Hints

 Other links

 Student comments

Number revision

www.samlearning.com

 This link takes you to the homepage. On the left-hand side of the screen click **KS3 SATs**, then choose **Maths** and then **Free Sample**.

 This is one of the best sites to visit for SATs exam practice but it's not free. You can only visit two areas based on **Number** if your school hasn't purchased it.

 Only two areas to try, but you really must visit them. Choose **Revise** before going on to **Exam Practice**. This is the closest you'll get to genuine SATs-style questions. It's certainly worth printing these pages off for your revision folder.

 www.s-cool.co.uk
This site is intended for GCSE students but is still worth a look to get those vital key points to help with your revision.

How to use it

Look out for

Hints

Other links

Student comments

www.revise.it/reviseit/Content/GCSE/Maths

This link takes you to the maths GCSE homepage. You are offered the four main areas, so think about what you want to practise.

Even though this is a GCSE site aimed at Years 10–11 there is plenty to look at. As the site is a revision site, it isn't interactive or colourful but gives the facts you must know in note form. This means you don't have to read through lots of text, so it will save you time.

As you work through the site, take note of the little extras offered. It will automatically highlight keywords for you. At the end of each section there are problems for you to try and even tests for some of the topics. If you return to the homepage there is a section taking you to other key revision sites, which are also worth a visit.

How to use it
 Look out for
 Hints
 Other links
 Student comments

www.satmath.com

 A direct link to the American SAT Math home page. Click on the **Trial Area**.

 This site is dedicated to the American version of the SATs that you take in Year 9. It has a small free area, so why not try an American SAT exam by choosing **Drill Test**? You only get to choose **Test 1** but there are 25 questions to keep you busy.

 There are some very tricky questions but it is a multiple choice test, so that helps a little. Read the instructions carefully so that you will know how to fill in the form properly. You can also go into the **Diagnostic** area for more testing. This area will also highlight your weaknesses and show you what you need to practise.